أربعين عن القرآن الكريم

40 HADĪTH ON THE QUR'ĀN

Edited by,
A.B. al-Mehri

www.quranproject.org

Distributed by,
The Qur'ān Project Distribution Centre
7-8 The Arcade
Luton
Bedfordshire
LU4 8JE
United Kingdom

Tel: 0800 228 9421
Email: info@quranproject.org
www.quranproject.org

Cover Design: H. Jundi

CONTENTS PAGE

Editors Preface

This booklet is a collection of Prophetic narrations about the Qur'ān that are profound and deep in their connotations. The booklet has been entitled, '40 Hadith on the Qur'ān' – although the number of narrations included in the book far exceed forty in number. However, out of the whole collection, forty Hadith have been specifically numbered highlighting their importance, status and relevance to our times.

You are also able to download a free PDF version of this booklet at www.quranproject.org.

May Allah [swt] allow us to memorise, benefit and implement the words of the Prophet Muhammad ﷺ. O Allah, make us of those who are the People of the Qur'ān, who live by the Qur'ān, call to the Qur'ān, judge by the Qur'ān and who recite it, learn it and ponder over it night and day. O Allah let the Qur'ān be a Hujjah [proof] in our favour and not against us [ameen].

A.B. al-Mehri
The Qur'ān Project
Birmingham, U.K.

بسم الله الرحمن الرحيم

Chapter: The Magnificence, Grandeur and Superiority of the Qur'ān

1. The Prophet Muhammad ﷺ said, "The superiority of the speech of Allah compared to all other speech is like the superiority of Allah over His creation."

Source: Tirmidhee no. 2926 - حسن [Hasan]

وفضلُ كلامِ اللهِ على سائرِ الكلامِ كفضلِ اللهِ على خلقه

2. The Prophet Muhammad ﷺ said, "Every Prophet was given miracles because of which people believed, but what I have been given is Divine Inspiration which Allah has revealed to me. So I hope that my followers will outnumber the followers of the other Prophets on the Day of Resurrection."

مَا مِنَ الأَنْبِيَاءِ نَبِيٌّ إِلاَّ أُعْطِيَ مَا مِثْلُهُ آمَنَ عَلَيْهِ الْبَشَرُ، وَإِنَّمَا كَانَ الَّذِي أُوتِيتُ وَحْيًا أَوْحَاهُ اللَّهُ إِلَيَّ فَأَرْجُو أَنْ أَكُونَ أَكْثَرَهُمْ تَابِعًا يَوْمَ الْقِيَامَةِ

Source: Bukhari no. 4981, Muslim no. 152 - صحيح [Sahih]

The Prophet Muhammad ﷺ said, "Indeed Allah, through this Book, raises some peoples and lowers others."

إِنَّ اللَّهَ يَرْفَعُ بِهَذَا الْكِتَابِ أَقْوَامًا وَيَضَعُ بِهِ آخَرِينَ

Source: Muslim no. 996 - صحيح [Sahih]

Chapter: The Level of Prophethood

3. The Prophet Muhammad ﷺ said, "Whoever recites the Qur'ān secures knowledge of prophethood within his ribs [bosom], though Divine Revelation is not sent upon him. It does not befit one endowed with the Qur'ān that he should be indignant with those in anger, nor should he indulge in any act of ignorance with those who are ignorant, while the Speech of Allah is there in his chest."

من قرأ القرآنَ فقد استدرج النُّبوَّةَ بين جنبيْه غيرَ أنَّه لا يُوحَى إليه لا ينبغي لصاحبِ القرآنِ أن يجِدَ مع من وجَد ولا يجهلَ مع من جهِل وفي جوفِه كلامُ اللهِ

Source: Hakim, Targhib wa Tarhib no. 2/301 - صحيح [Sahih]

The Prophet Muhammad ﷺ said, "You will not come back to Allah with anything better than that which came from Him, i.e. the Qur'ān."

إنَّكم لا ترجِعون إلى اللهِ بشيءٍ أفضلَ ممَّا خرج منه يعني القرآنَ

Source: Mastadrik al-Hakim no. 2077 - صحيح [Sahih]

Chapter: Most Precise and Accurate

4. The Prophet Muhammad ﷺ said, "The most accurate and truthful speech is the Book of Allah [swt]"

إنَّ أصدقَ الحديثِ كتابُ اللَّهِ

Source: Nisa'i no. 1578 - صحيح [Sahih]

The Prophet Muhammad ﷺ said, Allah [swt] said, "I have sent you [O Prophet] in order to put you to test and put those to test through you. And I sent the Book to you which cannot be washed away by water, so that you may recite it while in the state of wakefulness and sleep.

إِنَّمَا بَعَثْتُكَ لأَبْتَلِيَكَ وَأَبْتَلِيَ بِكَ وَأَنْزَلْتُ عَلَيْكَ كِتَابًا لاَ يَغْسِلُهُ الْمَاءُ تَقْرَؤُهُ نَائِمًا وَيَقْظَانَ

Source: Hadith Qudsi, Muslim no. 2865a - صحيح [Sahih]

Chapter: The Qur'ān is Pure and Undistorted

Ibn Abbas said, "How can you ask the people of the Scriptures about their Books while you have Allah's Book [the Qur'ān] which is the most recent of the Books revealed by Allah, and you read it in its pure undistorted form?"

كَيْفَ تَسْأَلُونَ أَهْلَ الْكِتَابِ عَنْ كُتُبِهِمْ وَعِنْدَكُمْ كِتَابُ اللَّهِ أَقْرَبُ الْكُتُبِ عَهْدًا بِاللَّهِ، تَقْرَءُونَهُ مَحْضًا لَمْ يُشَبْ

Source: Bukhari no. 7522 - صحيح [Sahih]

Chapter: Reciting the Qur'ān is a Light for You

The Prophet Muhammad ﷺ said, "It is imperative for you to have Taqwa [fear/consciousness of Allah] for this is the accumulation of all good. And upon you is Jihad in the path of Allah for it is the monasticism of the Muslims. [Finally]...upon you is the Rememberance of Allah and the recitation of His Book, for it is light for you on earth and [a means by which] you will be mentioned in the Heavens."

عليكَ بتقوَى اللهِ ، فإنَّها جِماعُ كلِّ خيرٍ ، وعليكَ بالجهادِ في سبيلِ اللهِ ، فإنَّها رهبانيةُ المسلمينَ ، وعليكَ بذكرِ اللهِ وتلاوةِ كتابِه ، فإنَّهُ نورٌ لكَ في الأرضِ ، وذِكرٌ لكَ في السَّماءِ

Source: Targhib wa-Tarhib no. 4/24, Jami as-Sagheer no. 5495 - صحيح لغيره [Sahih]

Chapter: Having doubt in the Qur'ān is Kufr

5. The Prophet Muhammad ﷺ said, "…Having doubt in the Qur'ān is [kufr] disbelief…."

الْمِرَاءُ فِي الْقُرْآنِ كُفْرٌ

Source: Abu Dawud no. 4603 - حسن [Hasan]

Chapter: The Qur'ān - an Intercessor

The Prophet Muhammad ﷺ said, "Fasting and the Qur'ān will intercede for the slave on the Day of Judgement. Fasting will say, 'O My Lord! I prevented him from food and desires, so accept my intercession for him.' And the Qur'ān will say, 'I prevented him from sleep during the night, so accept my intercession for him.' ....thus they will intercede."

الصِّيامُ والقرآنُ يشفعان للعبدِ يومَ القيامةِ يقولُ الصِّيامُ أيْ ربِّ منعتُه الطَّعامَ والشَّهوةَ فشفِّعني فيه ويقولُ القرآنُ منعتُه النَّومَ باللَّيلِ فشفِّعني فيه قال فيشفعان

Source: Musnad Ahmad no. 6337 - صحيح [Sahih]

Chapter: The Qur'ān as your Leader – guides you to Paradise. Placing behind your back leads to Hell

6. The Prophet Muhammad ﷺ said, "The Qur'ān is an intercessor and it's intercession is accepted and its plea is believed. Whoever makes it lead him – it leads him to Paradise and whomsoever places it behind him [the result will be] he is dragged to the Fire."

Source: Ibn Hibban no. 124, - صحيح [Sahih]

القرآنُ شافعٌ مُشفَّعٌ ، وماحلٌ مُصدَّقٌ ، من جعله أمامه قاده إلى الجنَّة، ومن جعله خلفه ساقه إلى النَّارِ

Chapter: The Qur'ān is a Proof/Evidence in your Favour or against You

The Prophet Muhammad ﷺ said, "Cleanliness is half of faith and Alhamdulillah [Praise be to Allah] fills the scale, and Subhan Allah [Glory be to Allah] and Alhamdulillah [Praise be to Allah] fill upwhat is between the heavens and the earth, and prayer is a light, and charity is

الطُّهُورُ شَطْرُ الإِيمَانِ وَالْحَمْدُ لِلَّهِ تَمْلأُ الْمِيزَانَ . وَسُبْحَانَ اللَّهِ وَالْحَمْدُ لِلَّهِ تَمْلآنِ - أَوْ تَمْلأُ - مَا بَيْنَ السَّمَوَاتِ وَالأَرْضِ وَالصَّلاَةُ نُورٌ وَالصَّدَقَةُ بُرْهَانٌ وَالصَّبْرُ ضِيَاءٌ

proof [of one's faith] and patience is a brightness and the Qur'ān is a proof on your behalf or against you."

وَالْقُرْآنُ حُجَّةٌ لَكَ أَوْ عَلَيْكَ

Source: Muslim no. 223 - صحيح [Sahih]

Chapter: Ramadhan: The Month of Various Revelations

The Prophet Muhammad ﷺ said, "The Suhuf [scrolls] of Ibrahim were revealed on the 1st night of Ramadhan. The Torah was revealed on the 6th of Ramadhan. The Injeel [Gopel] was revealed on the 13th of Ramadhan. The Zabur on the 18th of Ramadhan. And the Qur'ān on the 24th of Ramdhan."

أنزلت صحف إبراهيم أول ليلة من شهر رمضان، و أنزلت التوراة لست مضت من رمضان، و أنزل الإنجيل بثلاث عشرة مضت من رمضان، و أنزل الزبور لثمان عشرة خلت من رمضان، وأنزل القرآن لأربع وعشرين خلت من رمضان

Source: Jami as-Sagheer, Suyuti no. 2734 - حسن [Hasan]

Chapter: The Best amongst the Muslims

7. The Prophet Muhammad ﷺ said, "The best of you are those who learn the Qur'ān and teach it."

Source: Bukhari no. 5027, Tirmidhee no. 2909 – صحيح [Sahih]

خيرُكم مَن تعلَّم القرآنَ وعلَّمه

8. The Prophet Muhammad ﷺ said, "Allah has His own people among mankind." They said: "O Messenger of Allah, who are they?" He said: "The people of the Qur'ān, the people of Allah and those who are closest to Him."'

Source: Ibn Majah no. 215 - حسن [Hasan]

إنَّ للَّه أَهْلينَ مِنَ النَّاسِ قَالُوا يَا رَسُولَ اللَّه مَنْ هُمْ قَالَ هُمْ أَهْلُ الْقُرْآنِ أَهْلُ اللَّهِ وَخَاصَّتُهُ

Jabir ibn Abdullah said, "Allah's Messenger ﷺ shrouded every two martyrs of Uhud in one piece of cloth and then he would ask, "Which of them knew more Qur'ān?" When one of them was pointed out he

أَنَّ رَسُولَ اللَّهِ صلى الله عليه وسلم كَانَ يَجْمَعُ بَيْنَ الرَّجُلَيْنِ مِنْ قَتْلَى أُحُدٍ فِي ثَوْبٍ وَاحِدٍ ثُمَّ يَقُولُ "

would put him first in the grave."

Source: Bukhari no. 1347 – صحيح [Sahih]

أَيُّهُمْ أَكْثَرُ أَخْذًا لِلْقُرْآنِ ". فَإِذَا أُشِيرَ لَهُ إِلَى أَحَدِهِمَا قَدَّمَهُ فِي اللَّحْدِ

Abdullah ibn Masood said, "The bearer of the Qur'ān should be known by his night when the people are sleeping; by his day when people are awake; by his sadness when people are joyous; by his weeping when people are laughing."

Source: Nawawi in Tibyan al-Adab fi Hamalatul Qur'ān

ينبغي لحامل القرآن أن يعرف بليله إذا الناس نائمون وبنهاره إذا الناس مفطرون وبحزنه إذا الناس يفرحون وببكائه إذا الناس يختالون

The Prophet Muhammad ﷺ said, "If anyone prays at night reciting regularly ten verses, he will not be recorded among the negligent [ghafileen]; if anyone prays at night and recites a hundred verses, he will be recorded among those who are devout [qaniteen] to Allah; and if anyone prays at night reciting one thousand verses, he will be re-

مَنْ قَامَ بِعَشْرِ آيَاتٍ لَمْ يُكْتَبْ مِنَ الْغَافِلِينَ وَمَنْ قَامَ بِمِائَةِ آيَةٍ كُتِبَ مِنَ الْقَانِتِينَ وَمَنْ قَامَ بِأَلْفِ آيَةٍ كُتِبَ مِنَ الْمُقْنْطَرِينَ

cieve an immeasurable amount of reward."

Source: Abu Dawud no. 1398 - صحيح [Sahih]

Chapter: Amongst all the Creation – Whose Faith is most astounding?

9. The Messenger of Allah ﷺ said, "Whose Faith [Iman] amongst the various creations astounds you?" They [the Companions] said, "The Angels" He said, "The Angels - Why would they not Faith [when they are with their Lord]" They [then] said, "The Prophets" He said, "The Prophets recieve revelation so how would they not believe?" They [then] said, "[Us] the Companions" He said, "The Companions whom are with the Prophets - so how would they not believe? - However the Faith of people which is amazing and astounding is those who come after you who find Books

أيُّ الخَلْقِ أَعْجَبُ إيمانًا ؟ قالوا : الملائكةُ . قال : الملائكةُ كَيْفَ لا يُؤْمِنُونَ ؟ ! قالوا : النبيُّونَ . قال : النبيُّونَ يُوحَى إليهِمْ فكيفَ لا يُؤْمِنُونَ ؟ ! قالوا : الصَّحابَةُ . قال : الصَّحابَةُ مع الأنبياءِ فكيفَ لا يُؤْمِنُونَ ؟ ! ولَكِنَّ أَعْجَبَ الناسِ إيمانًا : قومٌ يَجِيئُونَ من بَعْدِكُمْ فَيَجِدُونَ كتابًا مِنَ الوَحْيِ ؛ فَيُؤْمِنُونَ بِه ويَتَّبِعُونَه ، فَهُمْ

which has written in them revelation [the Qur'ān] - and hence they believe in it and obey and follow it - they are the ones whose Faith is [truly] astounding."

أَعْجَبُ الناسِ إيمانًا – أَوْ الخَلْقِ إيمانًا

Source: Bazzar no. 3/318, Silsilah Ahadeeth as-Saheehah no. 3215 - صحيح [Sahih]

Chapter: Legislation/Judgement belongs to Allah

10. The Messenger of Allah ﷺ sent Mu'adh to Yemen, so He ﷺ said: "How will you judge?" He said: "I will judge according to what is in Allah's Book." He said, "If it is not in Allah's Book?" He said: "Then with the Sunnah of the Messenger of Allah ﷺ" He said: "If it is not in the Sunnah of Messenger of Allah ﷺ?" He said: "I will endevour to make Ijtihad [exert effort to make the correct judgement]." He said: "All praise is due to Allah, the One Who

أَنَّ رَسُولَ اللَّه صلى الله عليه وسلم بَعَثَ مُعَاذًا إِلَى الْيَمَنِ فَقَالَ "كَيْفَ تَقْضِي " . فَقَالَ أَقْضِي بِمَا فِي كِتَابِ اللَّه . قَالَ " فَإِنْ لَمْ يَكُنْ فِي كِتَابِ اللَّه " . قَالَ فَبِسُنَّةِ رَسُولِ اللَّه صلى الله عليه وسلم . قَالَ " فَإِنْ لَمْ يَكُنْ فِي سُنَّةِ رَسُولِ اللَّهِ صلى الله عليه

made the messenger of the Messenger of Allah suitable."
Source: Tirmidhee no. 1327

وسلم " . قَالَ أَجْتَهِدُ رَأْيِي . قَالَ " الْحَمْدُ لِلَّهِ الَّذِي وَفَّقَ رَسُولَ رَسُولِ اللَّهِ صلى الله عليه وسلم

Chapter: In-fighting when Leaders do not Rule by the Qur'ān

The Messenger of Allah ﷺ said, "O Muhajirun, there are five things with which you will be tested, and I seek refuge with Allah lest you live to see them: Immorality never appears among a people to such an extent that they commit it openly, but plagues and diseases that were never known among the predecessors will spread among them. They do not cheat in weights and measures but they will be stricken with famine, severe calamity and the oppression of their rulers. They do not withhold the Zakah of their wealth, but rain will be withheld

يَا مَعْشَرَ الْمُهَاجِرِينَ خَمْسٌ إِذَا ابْتُلِيتُمْ بِهِنَّ وَأَعُوذُ بِاللَّهِ أَنْ تُدْرِكُوهُنَّ لَمْ تَظْهَرِ الْفَاحِشَةُ فِي قَوْمٍ قَطُّ حَتَّى يُعْلِنُوا بِهَا إِلاَّ فَشَا فِيهِمُ الطَّاعُونُ وَالأَوْجَاعُ الَّتِي لَمْ تَكُنْ مَضَتْ فِي أَسْلاَفِهِمُ الَّذِينَ مَضَوْا . وَلَمْ يَنْقُصُوا الْمِكْيَالَ وَالْمِيزَانَ إِلاَّ أُخِذُوا بِالسِّنِينَ وَشِدَّةِ الْمَؤُنَةِ وَجَوْرِ السُّلْطَانِ عَلَيْهِمْ . وَلَمْ يَمْنَعُوا زَكَاةَ أَمْوَالِهِمْ إِلاَّ مُنِعُوا الْقَطْرَ

from the sky, and were it not for the animals, no rain would fall on them. They do not break their covenant with Allah and His Messenger, but Allah will enable their enemies to overpower them and take some of what is in their hands. Unless their leaders rule according to the Book of Allah and seek all good from that which Allah has revealed, Allah will cause them to fight one another."

Source: Ibn Majah no. 4019 - صحيح [Sahih]

مِنَ السَّمَاءِ وَلَوْلَا الْبَهَائِمُ لَمْ يُمْطَرُوا
وَلَمْ يَنْقُضُوا عَهْدَ اللَّهِ وَعَهْدَ رَسُولِهِ
إِلَّا سَلَّطَ اللَّهُ عَلَيْهِمْ عَدُوًّا مِنْ
غَيْرِهِمْ فَأَخَذُوا بَعْضَ مَا فِي
أَيْدِيهِمْ . وَمَا لَمْ تَحْكُمْ أَئِمَّتُهُمْ
بِكِتَابِ اللَّهِ وَيَتَخَيَّرُوا مِمَّا أَنْزَلَ اللَّهُ
إِلَّا جَعَلَ اللَّهُ بَأْسَهُمْ بَيْنَهُمْ

Chapter: Importance of Studying and Teaching the Qur'ān

11. The Prophet Muhammad ﷺ said, "This Qur'ān is the Banquet of Allah. Learn as much as you can from His banquet. This Qur'ān is the Rope of Allah, and it is the clear Light and [the effective and beneficial] Healing. It is a protection for the one who clings to it and a rescue for the one who follows it. It is not crooked and so puts things straight. It does not deviate so as to be blamed. It's wonders do not cease. It does not wear out with much repetition. So recite it for Allah will reward you for the recitation of every letter...." [also Abdullah ibn Masud said, 'This Qur'ān is the Banquet of Allah. Whoever enters it is safe.']

Source: Hakim no. 1/555, Darimi - صحيح [Sahih]

إنَّ هذا القرآنَ مَأْدُبَةُ اللهِ فتَعَلَّموا مَأْدُبَتَه ما استطعتم وإنَّ هذا القرآنَ هو حبلُ اللهِ وهو النورُ المبينُ والشفاءُ النافعُ عِصْمَةٌ مَن تَمَسَّك به ونجاةُ مَن تَبَعَه لا يَعْوَجُّ فيُقَوَّمُ ولا يَزِيغُ فيُسْتَعْتَبُ ولا تَنْقَضِي عجائبُه ولا يَخْلَقُ عن كَثْرَةِ الرَّدِّ اتلُوه فإنَّ اللهَ يأجرُكم على تلاوتِه بكلِّ حرفٍ

Qurtubi in his introduction to his tafseer quotes an explaination to this hadeeth as, '[the Banquet] is a metaphor. The Qur'ān is likened to something Allah has prepared for people. They have good and benefits in it. Then He has invited them to it.'

12. The Prophet Muhammad ﷺ said, "...A group of people do not gather in a house amongst the Houses of Allah [i.e. Masjid] reciting the Book of Allah and studying it between themselves – except that tranquillity descends upon them, they are enveloped by mercy and surrounded by the angels – and Allah mentions them with those with Him. [i.e. the higher angels]

Source: Muslim no. 9/1023, Abu Dawud no. 1455 - صحيح [Sahih]

وما اجتمعَ قومٌ في بيتٍ من بيوتِ اللهِ ، يتلون كتابَ اللهِ ، ويتدارسونه بينهم ، إلا نزلتْ عليهم السكينةُ ، وغشيتْهم الرحمةُ وحفّتهم الملائكةُ ، وذكرَهم اللهُ فيمن عنده

Qurtubi quotes a saying in his tafseer, "The metaphor of those who recite the Qur'ān without knowing its tafsir [explanation] is that of some people to whom a letter comes from their king at night when they have no lamp. They are alarmed, not knowing what the letter contains. The metaphor of the one who knows the tafsir [explanation] is that of a man who brings them a lamp so that they can read what the letter says."

The Prophet Muhammad ﷺ said, "Whoever teaches one verse of the Book of Allah Almighty, he will be rewarded [every time] it is recited."
Source: Silsilah Ahadeeth as-Saheehah no. 1335 - صحيح [Sahih]

من علمَ آيةً من كتابِ اللهِ عز وجل ، كانَ لهُ ثوابُها ما تليتْ

Chapter: Parents Honoured due to a Child's Relationship with the Qur'ān

13. The Prophet Muhammad ﷺ said, "Whoever recited the Qur'ān, studied it, and acted according to what it contains; on the Day of Judgment his parents will be dressed with a crown of light, its brightness is like that of

من قرأ القرآنَ وتعلّم وعمِل به أُلْبِس والداه يومَ القيامةِ تاجًا من نورٍ ضوءُه مثلُ الشَّمسِ ويُكسَى والداه حُلَّتَيْن لا يقومُ لهما الدُّنيا

the sun. And his parents will be adorned with two bracelets, of which the whole world is not equivalent to them [in worth]. So they will say, 'Why are we being adorned with these?' It will be said, 'This is because of your child taking [the recitation, teaching and acting upon] the Qur'ān."

Source: Hakim, Targhib wa Tarhib - صحيح [Sahih]

فيقولان بِمَ كُسينا هذا فيُقالُ بأخذِ ولدِكما القرآنَ

Chapter: A Warning Not to Learn the Qur'ān From....

14. The Prophet Muhammad ﷺ said, "Learn [study] the Qur'ān, and ask Allah [swt] to grant you Paradise by it, before when there comes people who learn it and ask by it, the worldy pleasures. Indeed, the Qur'ān is learnt by three types of people:

- A man who shows off by it
- A man who eats by it [money, dunyah]

تَعَلَّمُوا القرآنَ ، و سَلوا اللهَ به الجنةَ ، قبلَ أنْ يَتَعَلَّمُهُ قومٌ ، يَسْأَلونَ به الدنيا ، فإنَّ القرآنَ يَتَعَلَّمُهُ ثلاثَةٌ : رجلٌ يُباهِي بهِ ، و رجلٌ يَسْتَأْكِلُ بهِ ، و رجلٌ يقرأُهُ للَّهِ

- A man who recites it for the sake of Allah [swt]."

Source: Baihaqi, Shu'b al-Iman no. 2405 - صحيح [Sahih]

15. The Prophet Muhammad ﷺ said, "Read the Qur'ān and act by it. And do not abandon it, do not exceed it's limits, do not eat with it [i.e. money] and do not seek more by using it."

Source: Variation quoted by Nawawi in *Tibyan*, Sahih al-Jami no. 1168 - صحيح [Sahih]

اقرؤوا القرآنَ و اعملوا به ، و لا تَجْفُوا عنه ، و لا تغْلوا فيه ، و لا تأْكلوا به ، و لا تسْتَكثروا به

Chapter: A Warning to those who Misuse the Qur'ān and have an Incorrect/Corrupt Intention

16. The Prophet Muhammad ﷺ said, "[on the Day of Judgement]...and a man who acquired knowledge and taught others, and read Qur'ān. He will be brought, and Allah will remind him of His blessings, and he will acknowledge them. He [swt] will say, 'What did you do with them?' He will say, 'I ac-

ورجُلٌ تعلَّم العِلمَ وعلَّمه وقرَأ القرآنَ. فأُتِي به. فعرَّفه نِعَمَه فعرَفها. قال: فما عملتَ فيها ؟ قال: تعلَّمتُ العِلمَ وعلَّمتُه وقرَأتُ فيكَ القرآنَ. قال: كذَبتَ ولكنَّك

quired knowledge and taught others, and read the Qur'ān for Your sake.' He [swt] will say, 'You are lying. You acquired knowledge so that it would be said that you were a scholar; and you read Qur'ān so that it would be said that you were a Reciter, and it was said.' Then He will order that he be dragged on his face and thrown into the Fire."

Source: Muslim no. 1905a - صحيح [Sahih]

تعلَّمتَ العلمَ لِيُقالَ عالمٌ. وقرأتُ القُرآنَ لِيُقالَ هو قارئٌ. فقد قيل. ثم أمَرَ به فسُحِبَ على وجهه حتى أُلقي في النارِ

Chapter: A Warning to those who interpret the Qur'ān Insincerely – without Knowledge and merely following their personal views

17. The Prophet Muhammad ﷺ said, "Whoever says [something] about the Qur'ān without knowledge, then let him take his seat in the Fire."

Source: Tirmidhee no. 2950 - حسن [Hasan]

مَنْ قَالَ فِي الْقُرْآنِ بِغَيْرِ عِلْمٍ فَلْيَتَبَوَّأْ مَقْعَدَهُ مِنَ النَّارِ

The Prophet Muhammad ﷺ said, "And whoever says [something] about the Qur'ān according to his [own] opinion, then let him take his seat in the Fire."
Source: Tirmidhee no. 2951 - حسن [Hasan]

وَمَنْ قَالَ فِي الْقُرْآنِ بِرَأْيِهِ فَلْيَتَبَوَّأْ مَقْعَدَهُ مِنَ النَّارِ

Chapter: Argumentation

The Prophet Muhammad ﷺ said, "Do not argue in the Qur'ān [meaning do not oppose/argue against what the Qur'ān says] for in this arguing is Disbelief"
Source: Jami as-Sagheer no. 9739 - صحيح [Sahih]

لا تجادلوا في القرآنِ، فإنَّ جدالًا فيه كفرٌ

The Prophet Muhammad ﷺ said, "Do not argue using the Qur'ān [i.e. in a dispute with one another]. [The negative result would be] you would deny the Book of Allah by using [one ayat] against another [ayat]. I swear by Allah indeed the Believer if he is argued against with

لا تُجادلوا بالقرآنِ ، ولا تُكَذِّبوا كتابَ الله بعضَه ببعضٍ ؛ فوالله ! إنَّ المؤمنَ لَيُجادلُ بالقرآنِ فيُغلَبُ ، وإنَّ المنافقَ لَيُجادلُ بالقرآنِ

فَيَغلِبُ

the Qur'ān he [out of respect] will loose [not continue the argument]...indeed the hypocrite, if he argues using the Qur'ān, he will win [the argument – because the Believer will not argue back].

Source: Silsilah Ahadeeth as-Saheehah no. 3447 - صحيح [Sahih]

إنَّ ما أتخوَّفُ عليكم رجُلٌ قرأَ) القُرآنَ حتَّى إذا رُئِيَتْ بهجتُه عليه وكان رِدْئًا للإسلامِ غيَّره إلى ما شاء اللهُ فانسلَخ منه ونبَذه وراءَ ظَهرِهِ وسعى على جارِه بالسَّيفِ ورماه بالشِّركِ) قال : قُلْتُ : يا نبيَّ اللهِ أيُّهما أَوْلى بالشِّركِ المَرْميُّ أم الرَّامي ؟ قال : (بلِ الرَّامي

The Prophet Muhammad ﷺ said, "Indeed what I fear most for you all is that a man recites the Qur'ān until you can see the effects on his face [enlightened] and he will be like a shield for Islam by the permission of Allah, then he detatches himself [from the Qur'ān], he 'threw' it behind himself and he rushed upon his neighbour with the sword and he will accuse him of Shirk [polytheism]."

One of the companions said "O Prophet of Allah which of them will be the polytheist, the accuser or the one accused? He ﷺ said, "The accuser."

Source: Ibn Hibban no. 81 - صحيح [Sahih]

Chapter: *Taddabbur* [Pondering] on the Deep Meanings of the Qur'ān

Hasan al-Basri [one of the Tabi'een] said, "There was not revealed a [single] Ayat from the Qur'ān except that it has a Dhahir [an apparent] and Batin [inner] and every letter has a value [measure] – and for every value is an ending."

Source: Baghawi, Sharh us Sunnah no. 1/214

ما نزلَ من القرآنِ آيةٌ إلا لها ظهرٌ وبطنٌ ولكلِّ حرفٍ حدٌّ ولكلِّ حدٍّ مطلعٌ

Abdullah ibn Masood, the Companion, said, "When you intend to acquire knowledge, deeply study the Qur'ān for in it lies the [principles] of knowledge of the ancients and future generations."

Source: Ghazali, Kitab Adab Tilawat ul Qur'ān

وقال ابن مسعود إذا أردتم العلم فانثروا القرآن فإن فيه علم الأولين والآخرين

Hasan ibn Ali said, "The people before you considered the Qur'ān to be correspondence from their Lord, so they would ponder it by night and perform it by day."
Source: Nawawi, Tibyan fi Adab Hamalatul Qur'ān

إن من كان قبلكم رأوا القرآن رسائل من ربهم فكانوا يتدبرونها بالليل ويتفقدونها في النهار

Aishah said, "The Prophet ﷺ spent the night [in prayer] with [a single verse] Ayah from the Qur'ān."
Source: Tirmidhee no. 448 - صحيح [Sahih]

قَامَ النَّبِيُّ صلى الله عليه وسلم بِآيَةٍ مِنَ الْقُرْآنِ لَيْلَةً

Ibn Taymiyah said, "Whoever contemplates [tadabbur] upon the Qur'ān [with the condition] of seeking guidance from it, [then] the path of truth will be made clear."
Source: Aqeedah tul Wasityah

من تدبر القرآن طالبا الهدى منه؛ تبين له طريق الحق

Chapter: Etiquettes and Virtues of Reciting the Qur'ān

18. The Prophet Muhammad ﷺ said, "Allah listens more attentively to a man with a beautiful voice who recites Qur'ān out loud than the master of a singing slave-girl listens to his slave."

لَلَّهُ أَشَدُّ أَذَنًا إِلَى الرَّجُلِ الحَسَنِ الصَّوْتِ بِالقُرْآنِ يَجْهَرُ بِهِ مِنْ صَاحِبِ القَيْنَةِ إِلَى قَيْنَتِهِ

Source: Ibn Majah no. 1340, Ibn Hibban no. 754 - صحيح [Sahih – according to Ibn Hibban, Suyuti and Ibn Taymiyah]

19. The Prophet Muhammad ﷺ said, "Beautify the Qur'ān with your voices for indeed the nice voice increases the beauty of the Qur'ān"

حسِّنوا القرآنَ بأصواتِكم ؛ فإنَّ الصَّوتَ الحسنَ يزيدُ القرآنَ حُسنًا

Source: Baihaqi – Shu'bul Iman no. 2/868 - صحيح [Sahih]

20. The Prophet Muhammad ﷺ said, "Whoever recites a letter from Allah's Book, then he receives the reward from it, and the reward of ten the like of it. I

مَنْ قَرَأَ حَرْفًا مِنْ كِتَابِ اللَّهِ فَلَهُ بِهِ حَسَنَةٌ وَالْحَسَنَةُ بِعَشْرِ أَمْثَالِهَا لاَ أَقُولُ الم حَرْفٌ وَلَكِنْ أَلِفٌ حَرْفٌ

do not say that Alif Lam Mim is a letter, but Alif is a letter, Lam is a letter and Mim is a letter."

وَلاَمٌ حَرْفٌ وَمِيمٌ حَرْفٌ

Source: Tirmidhee no. 2910 - حسن [Hasan]

The Prophet Muhammad ﷺ said, "The one who does not recite the Qur'ān in a melodious manner is not from us"

ليس منا من لم يتغنَّ بالقرآنِ

Source: Bukhari no. 7527 - صحيح [Sahih]

21. The Prophet Muhammad ﷺ said, "...Recite the Qur'ān in [your houses]. For the inhabitants of the heavans see them like people on earth see the stars."

لَيُتْلَى فيهِ القرآنُ ، فيتراءَ لأهلِ السَّماءِ كما تَتَرَاءَى النُّجُومُ لأهلِ الأرضِ

Source: Syar Alam an-Nubalah, Dhahabi no. 8/29, Silsilah Ahadeeth as-Saheehah no. 3112 - صحيح [Sahih]

22. The Prophet Muhammad ﷺ said, "Purify [clean] your mouths with the siwak [tooth-stick] for indeed it [the mouth]

طيبوا أفواهكم بالسواكِ فإنها طرقُ

is the pathway of the Qur'ān."
Source: Baihaqi – Shu'bul Iman no. 2/862 - صحيح [Sahih]

القرآنِ

The Prophet Muhammad ﷺ said, "The one who recites the Qur'ān loudly is like one who gives charity openly, and the one who recites the Qur'ān silently is like the one who gives charity in secret."
Source: an-Nisa'i no. 1663, - حسن [Hasan]

إنَّ الَّذي يَجْهَرُ بِالْقُرْآنِ كَالَّذي يَجْهَرُ بِالصَّدَقَةِ وَالَّذي يُسِرُّ بِالْقُرْآنِ كَالَّذي يُسِرُّ بِالصَّدَقَةِ

23. The Prophet Muhammad ﷺ said, "Indeed the best of people who recite is one whom when you hear his recitation you can see that he Fears Allah."
Source: Hiyatul Awliyah no. 4/21 - صحيح [Sahih]

إنَّ أحسنَ الناسِ قراءةً من إذا سمعتَه يقرأُ رأيتُ أنه يخشى اللهَ

The Prophet Muhammad ﷺ said, "The parable of the believer who recites the Qur'ān is that of a sweet citrus fruit, its fragrance is nice and its taste is nice. The parable of the believer who does not recite the Qur'ān is that of a date, it has no smell but its taste is sweet. The parable of the hypocrite who recites the Qur'ān is that of basil, its fragrance is nice but its taste is bitter. The parable of the hypocrite who does not recite the Qur'ān is that of the colocynth [bitter desert fruit], its smell is better and its taste is bitter."

Source: Tirmidhee no. 2865 - صحيح [Sahih]

مَثَلُ الْمُؤْمِنِ الَّذِي يَقْرَأُ الْقُرْآنَ
كَمَثَلِ الأُتْرُجَّةِ رِيحُهَا طَيِّبٌ
وَطَعْمُهَا طَيِّبٌ وَمَثَلُ الْمُؤْمِنِ الَّذِي
لاَ يَقْرَأُ الْقُرْآنَ كَمَثَلِ التَّمْرَةِ لاَ رِيحَ
لَهَا وَطَعْمُهَا حُلْوٌ وَمَثَلُ الْمُنَافِقِ
الَّذِي يَقْرَأُ الْقُرْآنَ كَمَثَلِ الرَّيْحَانَةِ
رِيحُهَا طَيِّبٌ وَطَعْمُهَا مُرٌّ وَمَثَلُ
الْمُنَافِقِ الَّذِي لاَ يَقْرَأُ الْقُرْآنَ كَمَثَلِ
الْحَنْظَلَةِ رِيحُهَا مُرٌّ وَطَعْمُهَا مُرٌّ

The Prophet Muhammad ﷺ said, "And recite the Qur'ān in the early dawn. Verily the recitation of the Qur'ān in the early dawn is ever witnessed [17:78]." The Prophet said, "It is witnessed by the angels of the night

(وَقُرْآنَ الْفَجْرِ إِنَّ قُرْآنَ الْفَجْرِ
كَانَ مَشْهُودًا) قَالَ " تَشْهَدُهُ
مَلاَئِكَةُ اللَّيْلِ وَمَلاَئِكَةُ النَّهَارِ

and the angels of the day."
Source: Tirmidhee no. 3135 - صحيح
[Sahih]

24. Abdullah ibn Amr says, Allah's Messenger ﷺ said to me, "Recite the whole Qur'ān in a month." I said, "But I have the power [to do more than that]." Allah's Messenger ﷺ said, "Then finish the recitation of the Qur'ān in seven days, and do not finish it in less than this period."
Source: Bukhari no. 5054 - صحيح
[Sahih]

اقْرَإِ الْقُرْآنَ فِي شَهْرٍ ". قُلْتُ إِنِّي أَجِدُ قُوَّةً حَتَّى قَالَ " فَاقْرَأْهُ فِي سَبْعٍ وَلاَ تَزِدْ عَلَى ذَلِكَ

The Prophet Muhammad ﷺ said, "Envy is not justified but in case of two persons only: one who, having been given [knowledge of] the Qur'ān by Allah, recites it during the night and day [and also acts upon it] and a man who, having been given wealth by God, spends it during

لا حسدَ إلا في اثنتَين : رجلٍ آتاه اللهُ القرآنَ . فهو يقوم به أناءَ الليلِ وآناءَ النهارِ . ورجلٍ آتاه اللهُ مالًا . فهو ينفقُه آناءَ الليلِ وآناءَ النهارِ

the night and the day [for the welfare of others. seeking the pleasure of their Lord]."
Source: Muslim no. 815a - صحيح [Sahih]

Chapter: Disturbing others whilst reciting the Qur'ān

25. The Prophet Muhammad ﷺ said, "When someone is in Salah [prayer] then they are in deep conversation with their Lord Almighty so you should see if anyone is engaged in this deep conversation with their Lord [i.e. Salah] and do not make your voices loud one over the other in your recitation [of the Qur'ān]."
Source: Musnad Ahmad no. 7/188 - حسن - [Hasan]

إن المصليَ يناجي ربَّه عزَّ وجلَّ فلينظرْ أحدُكم بما يناجي ربَّه ولا يجهرْ بعضُكم على بعضٍ بالقراءةِ

Chapter: The Prophet Muhammad's ﷺ Relationship with the Qur'ān

26. Bar'a said, "I heard the Prophet ﷺ reciting Surat at-Tin waz Zaitun [95: By the Fig and the Olive] in the Isha prayer and I have never heard anybody with a better voice or recitation than his."

Source: Bukhari no. 7546 - صحيح [Sahih]

سَمِعْتُ النَّبِيَّ صلى الله عليه وسلم يَقْرَأُ فِي الْعِشَاءِ {وَالتِّينِ وَالزَّيْتُونِ} فَمَا سَمِعْتُ أَحَدًا أَحْسَنَ صَوْتًا أَوْ قِرَاءَةً مِنْهُ

In describing the Prophet's recitation of the Qur'ān, one of the companions said, كَانَ يَمُدُّ مَدًّا "He [the Prophet] would extend his voice appropriately and clearly [every letter would be pronounced properly] – [Abu Dawud no. 1465 - صحيح [Sahih]

The Prophet Muhammad ﷺ said, "Allah does not listen so attentively to anything as He listens to the recitation of the Qur'ān by a Prophet who recites it well with a melodious and

ما أذِن اللهُ لشيءٍ كأَذنه لنبيٍّ حسنِ الصوتِ يتغنَّى بالقرآنِ يجهرُ به

audible voice."
Source: Muslim no. 793b – صحيح [Sahih]

27. "One of the Companions said, "I saw the Messenger of Allah ﷺ and he was praying - his chest sounded like boiling water due to [him] crying."
Source: Ibn Hibban no. 753 - صحيح [Sahih]

رَأَيْتُ رسولَ اللهِ صلَّى اللهُ عليه وسلَّم يُصلِّي وفي صدرِه أزيزٌ كأزيزِ المِرجَلِمِن البكاءِ

28. Abdullah ibn Masud said, "The Messenger of Allah ﷺ asked me to recite the Qur'ān." He said "Messenger of Allah, [how] should I recite to you whereas it has been sent down to you? He [the Prophet] said, "I desire to hear it from some-one else." "So I recited Surat an-Nisa [4] till I reached the verse: "How then shall it be when We shall bring from every people a witness and bring you against them as a witness?" [4:41]. I

قال لي رسولُ اللهِ صلَّى اللهُ عليهِ وسلَّمَ " اقرأْ عليَّ القرآنَ " قال فقلتُ : يا رسولَ اللهِ ! أقرأُ عليك ، وعليك أُنْزِلَ ؟ قال " إني أشتهي أن أسمعَه من غيري " فقرأتُ النساءَ . حتى إذا بلغتُ : فَكَيْفَ إِذَا جِئْنَا مِنْ كُلِّ أُمَّةٍ بِشَهِيدٍ وَجِئْنَا بِكَ عَلَى هَؤُلَاءِ

lifted my head or a person touched me in my side, and so I lifted my head and saw his tears falling [from the Prophet's eyes].
Source: Muslim no. 800a - صحيح [Sahih]

شَهِيدًا [4 / النساء / الآية - 41] . رفعتُ رأسي . أو غمزَني رجلٌ إلى جنبي فرفعتُ رأسي . فرأيتُ دموعَه تسيلُ

Chapter: The Prophetic Character

29. Someone asked Aishah, Mother of the Believers, "Tell me about the character of the Messenger of Allah ﷺ" She said, "Do you not read the Qur'ān?" I said: "Yes." Upon this she said: "The character of the Messenger of Allah ﷺ was the Qur'ān."He said: "I felt inclined to get up and not ask anything [further] till death [due to the answer being so profound]"
Source: Muslim no. 746a, an-Nisa'i no. 1601, - صحيح [Sahih]

فَقُلْتُ يَا أُمَّ الْمُؤْمِنِينَ أَنْبِئِينِي عَنْ خُلُقِ رَسُولِ اللَّهِ صلى الله عليه وسلم . قَالَتْ أَلَسْتَ تَقْرَأُ الْقُرْآنَ قُلْتُ بَلَى . قَالَتْ فَإِنَّ خُلُقَ نَبِيِّ اللَّهِ صلى الله عليه وسلم كَانَ الْقُرْآنَ . - قَالَ - فَهَمَمْتُ أَنْ أَقُومَ وَلاَ أَسْأَلَ أَحَدًا عَنْ شَىْءٍ حَتَّى أَمُوتَ

Chapter: Virtue of the Memorizers [hufadh] of the Qur'ān

30. The Prophet Muhammad ﷺ said, "It shall be said to the Companion of the Qur'ān, 'Recite [of what you have memorized] and rise up, recite [melodiously] as you would recite in the world. For indeed your rank shall be at the last Ayah [verse] you recite."
Source: Tirmidhee no. 2914 - حسن [Hasan]

يقالُ لِصاحبِ القرآنِ : اقرأْ و ارْتَقِ ، و رَتِّلْ كما كُنْتَ تُرَتِّلُ في الدنيا ، فإنَّ منْزِلَتَكَ عندَ آخرِ آيةٍ [كُنْتَ] تَقْرَأُ بِها

The Prophet Muhammad ﷺ said, "The one who learns the Qur'ān is like the owner of a hobbled camel. If he pays attention to it, he will keep it, but if he releases it, it will go away."
Source: Bukhari no. 5031 - صحيح [Sahih]

إنَّ مَثَلَ صاحبِ القُرآنِ مَثَلُ صاحبِ الإبلِ المُعقَّلةِ إنْ عاهَدَ عليها عقَلها وإنْ أطلَقها ذهَبَتْ

31. The Prophet Muhammad ﷺ said, "It is a bad thing that some of you say, 'I have forgotten such-and-such verse of the

بِئْسَ مَا لأَحَدِهِمْ أَنْ يَقُولَ نَسِيتُ آيَةَ كَيْتَ وَكَيْتَ بَلْ نُسِّيَ، وَاسْتَذْكِرُوا الْقُرْآنَ فَإِنَّهُ أَشَدُّ تَفَصِّيًا

Qur'ān,' for indeed, he has been caused [by Allah] to forget it. So you must keep on reciting the Qur'ān because it escapes from the hearts of men faster than camel do."

مِنْ صُدُورِ الرِّجَالِ مِنَ النَّعَمِ

Source: Bukhari no. 5032 - صحيح [Sahih]

Abdullah ibn Masood, the Companion said, "It was difficult for us to memorise the words of the Qur'ān but easy for us to act by them. After us will be people for whom it is easy to memorise the Qur'ān, but hard to act by it."

إنا صعب علينا حفظ ألفاظ القرآن وسهل علينا العمل به ، ومن بعدنا يسهل عليهم حفظ القرآن ويصعب عليهم العمل به

Chapter: Not using Memorized Ayat in the Prayer causes forgetfulness

32. The Prophet Muhammad ﷺ said, "When the Companion of the Qur'ān performs Salah, reciting it by night and day, he retains it and if he doesn't [use it in] Salah he forgets."

إذا قام صاحبُ القرآنِ فقرأه باللَّيلِ والنَّهارِ ذكره ، وإن لم يقُمْ به نسِيه

Source: Silsilah Ahadeeth as-Saheehah no. 597 - صحيح [Sahih]

Chapter: Holding on to the Qur'ān - Never go Astray

33. The Prophet Muhammad ﷺ said, "...And I have left you two heavy [important issues]: The first of them is the Book of Allah. In it is the Guidance and the Light. Whoever holds firmly to it and takes from it he [then] is upon the Guidance. Whoever errs with respect to it goes astray. So take from the Book of Allah Almighty and hold firmly to it. [the second thing] is Ahl – Bayti [My Family – included wives, children, son-in law etc] I remind you by Allah with regard to My Family, I remind you by Allah with regard to My Family.
Source: Muslim, Ryadh as-Saliheen no. 346, – صحيح [Sahih]

وأنَا تاركٌ فيكمْ ثَقَلَيْنِ : أولُهما كتابُ الله فيه الهدى والنُّورُ، منْ استمسكَ به وأَخَذَ بهِ كانَ على الهُدى، ومنْ أخطأَهُ ضَلَّ، فخُذُوا بكتابِ الله تعالى، واسْتَمْسِكُوا بهِ؛ وأهلُ بيتِي، أذكِّرُكم اللهَ في أهلِ بيتِي، أذكِّرُكم اللهَ في أهلِ بيتِي

34. The Prophet Muhammad ﷺ said, "I leave behind for you, that by which if you stick firmly to you will never go astray, the Book of Allah and the Sunnah

إنِّي قد تركْتُ فيكم ما إنِ اعتصمتُمْ بهِ فلن تضلُّوا أبدًا كتابَ

of His Prophet." *Source:* Targhib wa Tarhib 1/61 صحيح [Sahih]	اللَّه وسنَّةَ نبيِّه
35. The Prophet Muhammad ﷺ said, "Indeed this Qur'ān is a rope – one end of it is in the Hand of Allah and the other end is in your hands. So hold firmly to it [the result would be] that you would never go astray and never be destroyed [no matter what the circumstance]." *Source:* Ibn Hibban no. 122 - صحيح [Sahih]	إنَّ هذا القرآنَ سببٌ طرفُه بيدِ الله ، و طرفُه بأيديكم ، فتمسَّكوا به ؛ فإنكم لن تضِلُّوا ولن تَهلِكوا بعده أبدًا

Chapter: The role of the Qur'ān in times of Fitnah [tribulation] and confusion

36. Ali said I heard the Messenger of Allah ﷺ says, 'Fitnah will certainly come.' I asked what is the way out O Messenger of Allah? He replied, 'The Book of Allah [swt] is the way, for it contains information of what happened before you, news of what will come after	ألَا إنَّها ستكونُ فتنةٌ ، فقلتُ : ما المَخرَجُ منها يا رسولَ الله ؟ قال : كتابُ الله فيه نَبَأُ ما قَبْلَكم ، وخَبَرُ ما بعدَكم ، وحُكْمُ ما بينكم ، وهو الفَصْلُ ليس بالهَزْلِ

you and a decision regarding matters that will occur among you....It is deciscive [fasl] and not a joke [hazl]. Whoever leaves leaves it, is a tyrant and Allah [swt] will break him, and if anyone seeks guidance elsewhere [other than the Qur'ān] Allah will lead him astray. It is the rope of Allah [swt], the wise reminder, the straight path, whims would not deviate it nor the tongue become confused, and the scholars cannot be fully satisfied [i.e. still more to explore]. It is not worn down by repetition nor do its wonders ever cease……He who quotes it speaks the truth, he who acts according to it is rewarded, he who judges according to it is just, and he who invites people to it [i.e. the Qur'ān] is [himself] guided to the Straight Path….'

Source: Tirmidhee no. 2906, ضعيف [إسناده مجهول] – [Da'eef - the chain is weak but the meaning is Saheeh –

مَن تركه من جَبَّارٍ قَصَمَهُ اللهُ ،
ومَن ابْتَغَى الهُدَى في غيرِه أَضَلَّهُ
اللهُ ، وهو حَبْلُ اللهِ المَتِينُ ، وهو
الذِّكْرُ الحكيمُ ، وهو الصراطُ
المستقيمُ . هو الذي لا تَزِيغُ به
الأهواءُ ، ولا تَلْتَبِسُ به الْأَلْسِنَةُ ،
ولا يَشْبَعُ منه العلماءُ ، ولا يَخْلَقُ
عن كَثْرَةِ الرَّدِّ ، ولا تَنْقَضِي
عجائبُه . هو الذي لم تَنْتَهِ الجِنُّ
إذ سَمِعَتْه حتى قالوا : إِنَّا سَمِعْنَا
قُرْآنًا عَجَبًا يَهْدِي إِلَى الرُّشْدِ فَآمَنَّا
به . مَن قال به صدق ، ومَن
عَمِلَ به أُجِرَ ، ومَن حكم به
عدل ، ومَن دعا إليه هُدِيَ إلى

scholars comment that this is more likely the statement of Ali and not the Prophet]

صراطٍ مستقيمٍ

Chapter: A Time will come when People will loose thc Understanding of the Qur'ān

37. On the authority of Ziyad ibn Lubayd the Prophet ﷺ said, '….and knowledge will go [or disappear].' He said, 'O Messenger of Allah how will knowledge leave [disappear] whilst we read the Qur'ān and our children read the Qur'ān and they will make their children read it till the Day of Judgement.' He ﷺ said, 'May your Mother loose you I thought your one of the men of understanding of Madinah. Don't you see these Jews and Christians reading their Torah and Gospel but they don't practice anything of it.'

Source: Ibn Majah no. 4048 - صحيح [Sahih]

وعن زياد بن لبيد قال ذكر النبي صلى الله عليه و سلم شيئا فقال : " ذاك عند أوان ذهاب العلم " قلت : يا رسول الله وكيف يذهب العلم ونحن نقرأ القرآن ونقرئه أبناءنا ويقرؤه أبناؤنا أبناءهم إلى يوم القيامة قال : " ثكلتك أمك زياد إن كنت لأراك من أفقه رجل بالمدينة أوليس هذه اليهود والنصارى يقرءون التوراة والإنجيل لا يعملون بشيء مما فيهما

38. The Prophet Muhammad ﷺ said, "There will come a time on the people when there will remain nothing of the Islam except its [*ism*] name and nothing will remain of the Qur'ān except its [*rasm*] outward form. Their masjids will be full of people/very well built but will be empty of guidance. Their scholars will be the most evil under the heavens; from them [*fitnah*] turmoil will emanate from them and to them will it return."

Source: Baihaqi, Shu'bul Iman no. 2/788

يوشك أن يأتي على الناس زمان لا يبقى من الإسلام إلا اسمه ولا يبقى من القرآن إلا رسمه مساجدهم عامرة وهي خراب من الهدى علماؤهم شر من تحت أديم السماء من عندهم تخرج الفتنة وفيهم تعود

Narrated Abdullah, that he heard a man reciting a Qur'ānic Verse which he had heard the Prophet reciting in a different way. So he took that man to the Prophet [and told him the story]. The Prophet said, "Both of you are reciting in a correct way, so carry on reciting." The

عَنْ عَبْدِ اللَّهِ، أَنَّهُ سَمِعَ رَجُلاً، يَقْرَأُ آيَةً، سَمِعَ النَّبِيَّ صلى الله عليه وسلم خِلاَفَهَا، فَأَخَذْتُ بِيَدِهِ فَانْطَلَقْتُ بِهِ إِلَى النَّبِيِّ صلى الله عليه وسلم فَقَالَ كِلاَكُمَا مُحْسِنٌ

Prophet ﷺ further added, "The nations which were before you were destroyed [by Allah] because they differed."

فَاقْرَآ . أَكْبَرُ عِلْمِي قَالَ . فَإِنَّ مَنْ كَانَ قَبْلَكُمْ اخْتَلَفُوا فَأَهْلَكَهُمْ

Source: Bukhari no. 5062 - صحيح [Sahih]

39. The Prophet Muhammad ﷺ said, "When you adorn [decorate] your Masajid and ornament your Qur'ān, then you will perish."

إذا زَخْرَفْتُم مَساجِدَكُم ، و حَلَّيْتُم مَصاحِفَكُم ، فالدَّمارُ عليكُمْ

Source: Jami as-Saghir no. 658 - حسن [Hasan]

40. The Prophet Muhammad ﷺ said, "The majority of the Hypocrites of this Ummah [Muslims] will be its readers [i.e. those who read the Qur'ān and not act according to it]."

أَكثرُ منافِقي هذهِ الأمَّةِ قرَّاؤُها

Source: Musnad Ahmad no. 10/123 - صحيح [Sahih]

An Amazing Prophetic Dua about the Qur'ān

O Allah make my heart flourish with the Qur'ān

اللّٰهُمَّ إِنِّي عَبْدُكَ ابْنُ عَبْدِكَ ابْنُ أَمَتِكَ نَاصِيَتِي بِيَدِكَ، مَاضٍ فِيَّ حُكْمُكَ، عَدْلٌ فِيَّ قَضَاؤكَ أَسْأَلُكَ بِكُلِّ اسْمٍ هُوَ لَكَ سَمَّيْتَ بِهِ نَفْسَكَ أَوْ أَنْزَلْتَهُ فِي كِتَابِكَ، أَوْ عَلَّمْتَهُ أَحَداً مِنْ خَلْقِكَ أَوِ اسْتَأْثَرْتَ بِهِ فِي عِلْمِ الغَيْبِ عِنْدَكَ أَنْ تَجْعَلَ القُرْآنَ رَبِيعَ قَلْبِي، وَنورَ صَدْرِي وَجَلَاءَ حُزْنِي وَذَهَابَ هَمِّي

"O Allah, I am Your servant, son of Your servant, son of Your maidservant, my forelock is in Your hand, Your command over me is forever executed and Your decree over me is just. I ask You by every name belonging to You which You named Yourself with, or revealed in Your Book, or You taught to any of Your creation, or You have preserved in the knowledge of the unseen with You, that You make the Qur'ān the spring of my heart [i.e. make my heart flourish with the Qur'ān] and the light of my chest, and a departure for my sorrow and a release for my anxiety."

Source: Musnad Ahmad no. 6/153, Ibn Hibban no. 972 - صحيح [Sahih]

Dua's from the Qur'ān

رَبَّنَا تَقَبَّلْ مِنَّا إِنَّكَ أَنْتَ السَّمِيعُ الْعَلِيمُ

"Our Lord, accept [this] from us. Indeed You are the Hearing, the Knowing." [2:127]

رَبَّنَا آتِنَا فِي الدُّنْيَا حَسَنَةً وَفِي الْآخِرَةِ حَسَنَةً وَقِنَا عَذَابَ النَّارِ

"Our Lord, give us in this world [that which is] good and in the Hereafter [that which is] good and protect us from the punishment of the Fire." [2:201]

رَبَّنَا أَفْرِغْ عَلَيْنَا صَبْرًا وَثَبِّتْ أَقْدَامَنَا وَانْصُرْنَا عَلَى الْقَوْمِ الْكَافِرِينَ

"Our Lord, pour upon us patience and plant firmly our feet and give us victory over the disbelieving people." [2:250]

رَبَّنَا لَا تُؤَاخِذْنَا إِنْ نَسِينَا أَوْ أَخْطَأْنَا رَبَّنَا وَلَا تَحْمِلْ عَلَيْنَا إِصْرًا كَمَا حَمَلْتَهُ عَلَى الَّذِينَ مِنْ قَبْلِنَا رَبَّنَا وَلَا تُحَمِّلْنَا مَا لَا طَاقَةَ لَنَا بِهِ وَاعْفُ عَنَّا وَاغْفِرْ لَنَا وَارْحَمْنَا أَنْتَ مَوْلَانَا فَانْصُرْنَا عَلَى الْقَوْمِ الْكَافِرِينَ

"Our Lord, do not impose blame upon us if we have forgotten or erred. Our Lord, and lay not upon us a burden like that which You laid upon those before us. Our Lord, and burden us not with that which we have no ability to bear. And pardon us; and forgive us; and have mercy upon us. You are our protector, so give us victory over the disbelieving people." [2:286]

رَبَّنَا لَا تُزِغْ قُلُوبَنَا بَعْدَ إِذْ هَدَيْتَنَا وَهَبْ لَنَا مِن لَّدُنكَ رَحْمَةً إِنَّكَ أَنتَ الْوَهَّابُ

"Our Lord, let not our hearts deviate after You have guided us and grant us from Yourself mercy. Indeed, You are the Bestower." [3:8]

رَبَّنَا إِنَّنَا آمَنَّا فَاغْفِرْ لَنَا ذُنُوبَنَا وَقِنَا عَذَابَ النَّارِ

"Our Lord, indeed we have believed, so forgive us our sins and protect us from the punishment of the Fire," [3:16]

رَبَّنَا آمَنَّا بِمَا أَنزَلْتَ وَاتَّبَعْنَا الرَّسُولَ فَاكْتُبْنَا مَعَ الشَّاهِدِينَ

"Our Lord, we have believed in what You revealed and have followed the messenger so register us among the witnesses [to truth]." [3:53]

رَبَّنَا اغْفِرْ لَنَا ذُنُوبَنَا وَإِسْرَافَنَا فِي أَمْرِنَا وَثَبِّتْ أَقْدَامَنَا وَانصُرْنَا عَلَى الْقَوْمِ الْكَافِرِينَ

"Our Lord, forgive us our sins and the excess [committed] in our affairs and plant firmly our feet and give us victory over the disbelieving people." [3:147]

رَبَّنَا مَا خَلَقْتَ هَٰذَا بَاطِلًا سُبْحَانَكَ فَقِنَا عَذَابَ النَّارِ

"Our Lord, You did not create this [heavens and earth] aimlessly; exalted are You [above such a thing]; then protect us from the punishment of the Fire." [3:191]

رَبَّنَا إِنَّنَا سَمِعْنَا مُنَادِيًا يُنَادِي لِلْإِيمَانِ أَنْ آمِنُوا بِرَبِّكُمْ فَآمَنَّا رَبَّنَا فَاغْفِرْ
لَنَا ذُنُوبَنَا وَكَفِّرْ عَنَّا سَيِّئَاتِنَا وَتَوَفَّنَا مَعَ الْأَبْرَارِ

"Our Lord, indeed we have heard a caller calling to faith, [saying], 'Believe in your Lord,' and we have believed. Our Lord, so forgive us our sins and remove from us our misdeeds and cause us to die with the righteous." [3:193]

رَبَّنَا أَخْرِجْنَا مِنْ هَٰذِهِ الْقَرْيَةِ الظَّالِمِ أَهْلُهَا وَاجْعَل لَّنَا مِن لَّدُنْكَ وَلِيًّا
وَاجْعَل لَّنَا مِن لَّدُنْكَ نَصِيرًا

"Our Lord, take us out of this city of oppressive people and appoint for us from Yourself a protector and appoint for us from Yourself a helper?" [4:75]

رَبَّنَا ظَلَمْنَا أَنفُسَنَا وَإِنْ لَّمْ تَغْفِرْ لَنَا وَتَرْحَمْنَا لَنَكُونَنَّ مِنَ الْخَاسِرِينَ

"Our Lord, we have wronged ourselves, and if You do not forgive us and have mercy upon us, we will surely be among the losers." [7:23]

رَبَّنَا أَفْرِغْ عَلَيْنَا صَبْرًا وَثَبِّتْ أَقْدَامَنَا وَانْصُرْنَا عَلَى الْقَوْمِ الْكَافِرِينَ

"Our Lord, accept [this] from us. Indeed You are the Hearing, the Knowing." [2:127]

رَبَّنَا لَا تَجْعَلْنَا مَعَ الْقَوْمِ الظَّالِمِينَ

"Our Lord, do not place us with the wrongdoing people." [7:47]

رَبَّنَا افْتَحْ بَيْنَنَا وَبَيْنَ قَوْمِنَا بِالْحَقِّ وَأَنْتَ خَيْرُ الْفَاتِحِينَ

"Our Lord, decide between us and our people in truth, and You are the best of those who give decision" [7:89]

رَبِّ اجْعَلْنِي مُقِيمَ الصَّلَاةِ وَمِنْ ذُرِّيَّتِي رَبَّنَا وَتَقَبَّلْ دُعَاءِ

"My Lord, make me an establisher of prayer, and [many] from my descendants. Our Lord, and accept my supplication." [14:40]

رَبَّنَا اغْفِرْ لِي وَلِوَالِدَيَّ وَلِلْمُؤْمِنِينَ يَوْمَ يَقُومُ الْحِسَابُ

"Our Lord, forgive me and my parents and the believers the Day the account is established." [14:41]

رَبَّنَا آتِنَا مِنْ لَدُنْكَ رَحْمَةً وَهَيِّئْ لَنَا مِنْ أَمْرِنَا رَشَدًا

"Our Lord, grant us from Yourself mercy and prepare for us from our affair right guidance." [18:10]

رَبَّنَا اصْرِفْ عَنَّا عَذَابَ جَهَنَّمَ إِنَّ عَذَابَهَا كَانَ غَرَامًا

"Our Lord, avert from us the punishment of Hell. Indeed, its punishment is ever adhering." [25:65]

رَبَّنَا هَبْ لَنَا مِنْ أَزْوَاجِنَا وَذُرِّيَّاتِنَا قُرَّةَ أَعْيُنٍ وَاجْعَلْنَا لِلْمُتَّقِينَ إِمَامًا

"Our Lord, grant us from among our wives and offspring comfort to our eyes and make us an example for the righteous." [25:74]

رَبَّنَا وَسِعْتَ كُلَّ شَيْءٍ رَحْمَةً وَعِلْمًا فَاغْفِرْ لِلَّذِينَ تَابُوا وَاتَّبَعُوا سَبِيلَكَ وَقِهِمْ عَذَابَ الْجَحِيمِ

"Our Lord, You have encompassed all things in mercy and knowledge, so forgive those who have repented and followed Your way and protect them from the punishment of Hell-fire." [40:7]

رَبَّنَا وَأَدْخِلْهُمْ جَنَّاتِ عَدْنٍ الَّتِي وَعَدْتَهُمْ وَمَنْ صَلَحَ مِنْ آبَائِهِمْ وَأَزْوَاجِهِمْ وَذُرِّيَّاتِهِمْ إِنَّكَ أَنْتَ الْعَزِيزُ الْحَكِيمُ وَقِهِمُ السَّيِّئَاتِ وَمَنْ تَقِ السَّيِّئَاتِ يَوْمَئِذٍ فَقَدْ رَحِمْتَهُ وَذَلِكَ هُوَ الْفَوْزُ الْعَظِيمُ

"Our Lord, and admit them to gardens of perpetual residence which You have promised them and whoever was righteous among their fathers, their spouses and their offspring. Indeed, it is You who is the Exalted in Might, the Wise.And protect them from the evil consequences [of their deeds]. And he whom You protect from evil consequences that Day - You will have given him mercy. And that is the great attainment." [40:8-9]

رَبَّنَا اغْفِرْ لَنَا وَلِإِخْوَانِنَا الَّذِينَ سَبَقُونَا بِالْإِيمَانِ وَلَا تَجْعَلْ فِي قُلُوبِنَا غِلًّا لِلَّذِينَ آمَنُوا رَبَّنَا إِنَّكَ رَءُوفٌ رَحِيمٌ

"Our Lord, forgive us and our brothers who preceded us in faith and put not in our hearts [any] resentment toward those who have believed. Our Lord, indeed You are Kind and Merciful." [59:10]

رَبَّنَا عَلَيْكَ تَوَكَّلْنَا وَإِلَيْكَ أَنَبْنَا وَإِلَيْكَ الْمَصِيرُ

"Our Lord, upon You we have relied, and to You we have returned, and to You is the destination."[60:4]

رَبِّ أَوْزِعْنِي أَنْ أَشْكُرَ نِعْمَتَكَ الَّتِي أَنْعَمْتَ عَلَيَّ وَعَلَى وَالِدَيَّ وَأَنْ أَعْمَلَ صَالِحًا تَرْضَاهُ وَأَصْلِحْ لِي فِي ذُرِّيَّتِي إِنِّي تُبْتُ إِلَيْكَ وَإِنِّي مِنَ الْمُسْلِمِينَ

"My Lord, enable me to be grateful for Your favor which You have bestowed upon me and upon my parents and to work righteousness of which You will approve and make righteous for me my offspring. Indeed, I have repented to You, and indeed, I am of the Muslims." [46:15]

رَبِّ أَعُوذُ بِكَ مِنْ هَمَزَاتِ الشَّيَاطِينِ وَأَعُوذُ بِكَ رَبِّ أَنْ يَحْضُرُونِ

"My Lord, I seek refuge in You from the incitements of the devils. And I seek refuge in You, my Lord, lest they be present with me." [23:97-98]

رَّبِّ ارْحَمْهُمَا كَمَا رَبَّيَانِي صَغِيرًا

"My Lord, have mercy upon them [my parents] as they brought me up [when I was] small." [17:24]

رَبِّ اغْفِرْ وَارْحَمْ وَأَنْتَ خَيْرُ الرَّاحِمِينَ

"My Lord, forgive and have mercy, and You are the best of the merciful." [23:118]

رَبِّ زِدْنِي عِلْمًا

"My Lord, increase me in knowledge." [20:114]

Notes & Useful Information

Notes & Useful Information

Notes & Useful Information

Notes & Useful Information

Notes & Useful Information

Printed in Great Britain
by Amazon

20251857R00038